# Blue Beginnings

Ashley Rafaela

Presentation by *BookLeaf Publishing*

Web: www.bookleafpub.com

E-mail: info@bookleafpub.com

ISBN: 9789357617482

First edition 2022

# A Type of Love

It's raining leaves today and the wind speaks through them like something deep, like something approaching old, and so I'm told, too beautiful to keep.

There's something we whisper to ourselves at night, when eyes close and life collapses in on itself, when time collapses in on itself, turning cavernous and wide, and we wonder why the words we whisper disintegrate sometimes, and we lose our step sometimes, we think we fall way too short sometimes.

But the wind that makes the leaves rain is whispering something sweet, up from the twisted bottom of things, and we feel the gentle pull of times before these when rivers ran free and bodies could sing. A tracing of love to the root, to hearts dipped in red, changing always changing, but never losing when the past is far from dead and things we've laid to rest come back instead. And what does death mean anyway, and what is loss anyway, when time stretches deep not wide and all the ghosts know us by name.

Hearts dipped in red, when they looked me in the eye and said they wouldn't change a single thing about me. A single thing about me, and I couldn't believe it and still can't believe it, but it's raining leaves today and some part of me believes it in the way that people can mean exactly what they say. And sometimes you don't look away and you stay. And isn't that a type of love, like something deep, like something approaching old, and so I'm told, too beautiful to keep.

# Laugh Me to My Knees

The light floats in and out from behind my eyes,
and I'm tired of looking, looking, looking.
Betting on hope with furtive glances. I take too
many chances and still not enough.

So much unlived life inside these bones, but I
feel okay today. I laughed the breath away, saw
light in your eyes come out to play, and so I feel
okay today.

Residual joy meets a gray sky and brushes it
with dancing leaves. With rustle-talk that near
brings me to my knees. Secrets being passed
underneath and all of a sudden, I feel like flying.
Fingertips grazing, soaring hazy. Secrets rustling
beneath. A small part of me understands, from
this place I expand, and all of a sudden, I feel
like flying.

So bring your wings and take me when you go.
Take me when your eyes close.
Breathe me the silence in between.
Sing me the waters underneath.
Kiss me the nothing that shakes the leaves.
And laugh me gently, gently to my knees.

# Bless Them On Their Way

There's magic in the air and it tussles round my hair, dark swimming snakes bending space. I can't see you, but I can feel you rising from my belly to my chest.

I had a dream we were sitting on a park bench and talking in the spaces beneath the air. Gentle fingertips pressing here, pressing there, tussling round my hair. Moments ripe and on their way to bruising.

Leave me alone, so I can see how much I've grown. I'm learning to focus on what I have, the sweetness of moments bursting, ripe and on their way to bruising. Losses ready the heart and teach it how to let things go into grace. Moments lived never in haste expand into forever, even as they seem to slip through grasping hands. Life remains in ways we can't explain. Moving in the spaces beneath the air. Tussling round our hair. Pressing here, pressing there.

There is no sun today. Autumn days reaching, rising from my belly to my chest. Melancholy visitors kissed by the sun and flying, dreams swept to the ground in a gentle dying. Yet something sweet remains, a new impression ingrained, a rearranging of the heart and all its parts. Everything is lost, while everything is gained. Kissed by the sun and let go into moving, moments ripe and on their way to bruising.

# The Heart That Allows

Look deep into my eyes and tell me you're afraid.

Nothing more to say than this. Seal your courage with a kiss. Nothing more to say than this.

What is love but a breaking and falling away with open arms? Trusting that wherever we land, we land whole, changed and unchanged, ready and not ready. Afraid and unafraid.

What is love but a witnessing, a deep and full body listening? No offense, but your labels just ain't it. Imperfection a myth of design, intelligence a rigid measure of time. Come what may, come what might. Impermanence a creature of the quiet night. Look deep into its eyes and tell it you're afraid.

Nothing more to say than this. Seal your courage with a kiss. Nothing more to say than this.

# Before the Blue

Slanted, angled light illuminates red impermanence, and I weep for all my joys and sorrows at once. You were beautiful when you kissed me with your voice, with your sigh weighted with cautious hope, escaped joy, fleeting, soaring up and down and away, into something else.

How many transformations start with a single breath, soaring up and down and away?

I've been dreaming since Thursday, for three hazy days. Your voice reached me through the phone, and I felt like I was still dreaming. Like I've had this dream before, but it's real in the way my skin buzzes when you talk.

You've kissed me with your voice before. You were beautiful then, before the water and the blue, before our bodies looked like this, before the mangos tasted sweet with our eyes and with our mouths. We were somewhere else, I forget, but what I remember is how I've always known you. Beautiful then and beautiful now. Dreaming

the real into waking, buzzing skin, your laugh a
hymn of cautious hope, joy escaped and fleeting.

I love you in a way I don't understand.
Something like water, something like blue. I
love you. If I can ever dream the real into
waking, I wouldn't change a thing. Even with
impermanence illuminated, angled light and
shifting shapes, I wouldn't change a thing.

Everything a flowing dream. Always changing, I
wouldn't change a thing.

# A Small Hill in Ohio

Tired eyes that hide, yet luminosity rises up in
unlikely moments, on unlikely days. No feeling
is ever here to stay and thank god for that, thank
god for that.

Can you count the alphabet backwards or am I
just full of shit? Take me to your favorite place
and show me why it shines for you, beauty in the
why and how of a thing. Why does it shine and
how does it rise up in unlikely moments, on
unlikely days?

My favorite part about your favorite place is the
way your shoulders relax down from your ears
when you're here, expelling fear with the breath,
inhaling wisdom near, just near enough to rest.

# All Colors Present

Something about the way a laugh sparkles over you, filtered light casting rainbows, punctured by the caw of a crow. All colors present.

Please do me the gentle favor of getting out of your own damn way. Light the path for the rest of us, away from pretending, away from being guided by fear, by shame, towards liberation and a most graceful integration of joy and pain. Drawing a circular breath that's real and true. All colors present.

Madre, I want to be someone who speaks and acts from the heart, filtered light, casting rainbows over the precious things I love. I want this list of precious things to grow deeper and wider every day, capacity for love growing impossibly large, widening out and over wounds, taking care, taking care. All colors present.

Did you know that the fleeting things are sacred? Sometimes I wonder what form of energy I'll take next and if I will still recognize and be recognized by the things I love. Maybe

you will be silence and I will be the crow that
punctures and deepens you as I sing. Maybe
we'll both have wings. Maybe we'll finally feel
free. Maybe we'll forget ourselves and our given
names. In that case, may our love ride the winds
long after, carrying seeds that will blush in
bloom to the shade. A crow and a caw away.
Feathered spirits clear the way. All colors
present.

# Dream Fragment

12

Your death will last a hundred years,
And it will be beautiful,
And sometimes it won't even feel like dying.

# Healing Words

Mija, you are worth knowing.

If you let go into anything, let go into that.

# Joy Enough

The day passes over and into our hearts. Say it once and say it again.

Yesterday, a small boy swung his arms up and down and around. Remember that at some point we still believed in flying, or at least in trying. The possibility was joy enough. Liberation is following the pull of curiosities just for the sake of it, the mysterious take of it. Everything now is joy enough.

What if we're the wizards we've been waiting for, magic making a choice we take, a path we rake, a discipline of awe we never forsake through the porousness of our being. Laughter spills and tears fill otherwise empty spaces. Look upon all these faces and tell me there's not a billion stories there, written in memories that change a little each day, but the texture remains the same.

Small arms swing through alive sky, knowing some things we see not with eyes, but with a porousness of all our senses. What part of the boy remembers flying? The possibility is joy enough. The mysterious take of it. Laugh for the sake of it. Cry for the weight of it. Sing just to prove you can. Just another version of flying. Magic rising. The possibility is joy enough. A choice we make. Everything now is joy enough.

# Buoyant Parts

To have a heart that sings in strings. I've never met you, but I've sung you on my tongue. The subtle sweetness made me dream about a clear blue sea and other forgotten things. So clearly I could see, so clearly I could see.

Have you ever noticed we both have eyes that pool in piles of rich dark earth? If you look closely enough, you'll see the etchings of majestic trees, rooted kings swimming in the shells of scattered, floating seeds. Trees for eyes. Buoyant parts to start. I trust the taste of you in the dark. Rooted kings and strings for hearts.

# Sorrows Out to Rise

Ache me like a violin.
Bake me like a cake.
Steam my sorrows out to rise,
Vapor-like through passages deep and wide.

Sometimes beauty emerges from the edges,
sparkling out from darkness, soft and blurred,
but there, so very much there. I didn't mean to
hurt you. I love your heart. Do you believe me? I
love your heart.

I love our love like nothing else I've ever
known. Even as it transforms before our eyes,
growing away from old beloved shapes, even as
the heart breaks and tired voices shake like
strings. Vibrating aches with wings. Turning
sorrows into song, just help me feel like I
belong. Alive this time, not dreaming or halfway
dead. Alive this time. Let it be said. Not
dreaming or halfway dead.

I loved and will love again. Even once I'm dead.
I will love again. Resurrection from the edge.
Different, but the same. I will love again. Do
you believe me? I didn't mean to hurt you. Do
you believe? I didn't mean to hurt.

# Not the Body, the Light

I saw trees in your eyes, wind sweeping your hair up through the sky, reaching like branches towards the narrow edges of life itself.

What are edges but the frontiers from which old leaves are spun into new dreams? Fresh sight bursting through seams from the inside out. We outgrow ourselves again and again. The me that brewed a simple cup of coffee this morning is already an old, old friend. Past selves settling into rings, holding us firmly up as we expand and twist our way forward.

They said that we are the light that makes the shadow, not the body, but the light, and I can't say why, but it's beautiful and it means something. Perhaps the unexplainable is the closest truth we have. There's a way my heart grasps it, recognizes it. A quickening akin to love. A sense of belonging to life. To being creation and creator at once.

Madre, please lend me another day to work out these mysteries, the ones that glimmer out to me in the dark. Sometimes my heart beats in a way

that I become aware of myself as something
with rhythm, an instrument of some kind,
pulsing from inside, skin vibrating beyond itself,
nudging the air playfully, both an invitation and
familial recognition at once. Little drums that
beat. Little moments of peace dripping
candlewax heat over all stirring wild things.

# We Forget

Steeped in laurels from former days, it's well
past morning and the sun has yet to show her
face. Oh gentle grace, what if today was the day
of my awakening and I didn't know it, I just
didn't know it?

Tumble me down with the truth and don't let me
look away. Even the grayest days sing in rich
hues and sometimes beauty is a thing we choose.
A word we decide to say on colorless days.

Overcast with crows who carry our breath,
giving it flight. Sometimes we can even hear our
own selves flapping through the sinking night. Is
there such thing as creatures winged and not
free? Only when the memory of wings becomes
elusive as a dream. We forget, we forget, we
forget.

# Still Invested in the Sowing

Images seeping through as from nothing, blank pages revealing stoic faces with swimming eyes. So alive, causing my heart to expand, tight and glowing, impossibly big inside my chest. It's true that expansion can hurt, or at least cause discomfort in the growing.

Do you ever feel that we might be at the end, still invested in the sowing? I wonder what will bloom long after we've said goodbye. Will I ache for the way we used to be, soft and sweet? Will I recognize the way you changed me, the way our closeness still lives inside me? Soft and sweet.

The truth is there is no such thing as blank pages. Images don't seep through as from nothing. Nothing does not, cannot exist, and isn't that funny? Everything is something. Even nothing has a size and a shape. Take a blank page, a seed. Invisible and alive inside. Futures encased in the present soon to be the past.

Discomfort in the growing as nothing lasts. Even so, I let my heart be pulled by dark swimming eyes. So alive it hurts. So alive. It hurts. In a golden way. It hurts.

# The Heart Knows and We Can Only Wonder

There's a reason my heart still speaks, still weeps for pains of others. For pain both young and old, sharp and blunt, sparkling and rusty red.

There's a metallic taste on my tongue today and I want to slice evil away at the root. Rotten fruit fall where it may, is it terrible to say that some people may be beyond salvation in this lifetime? That in disregarding another's innocent humanity over and over, they have forfeited their own. Are as good as dead having set aside everything human inside them for lead. Heart unreachable. What, then? Madre, help me understand. What, then?

All I know is that there's a reason my heart still speaks. Sing me something sweet. Honey me up like golden leaves. Love me in a language I can understand. So much sorrow, it's a wonder, and yet…

# Sinking into Life

There are things I've noticed lately, drinking eyes. Murmurations sweeping in and out of cloudless sky. Crackling. Swooping. Jagged and unafraid. There is power in numbers, though the degree of intention counts for a lot. Matters. Who is pushing in? Who is pushing out? Travelers.

Some mornings I wake with a slight throbbing in the temples as the day rises up ahead, looming, impossibly big, like a shadow that swallows its source. To see the magician behind the screen, living for all that remains to be seen, tasted. Felt.

Eyes that drink, sipping.
Skin the melts, dripping.
Tongues that paint, making shapes.

Life requires your immediate observation. A less celebrated type of participation. Wondering minds turning answers into questions, questions into songs. Making more space, acquiring more grace, heart sinking into a more gentle pace.

# Blue Beginnings

Dust settles as sighs close in and around and out. The very things we swear to take to the grave come back, always back until we meet them eye to eye, soul to soul, seeing with resigned patience, the type that gifts moments deeper than tales we've never heard the end of. Tunnels to get lost in, soft in, get a mother fucking thought in. Please remind me not to take life for granted again. And again. Until my heart beats with dusk that rusts in smoky colors, different but the same, every night arrives with an altered but recognizable name.

Sometimes it's questions to an empty universe, but sometimes something breathes back and we listen in languages that can't be taught, from spaces that words can't touch. New beginnings are everywhere, as common as the stars, with just as magic in their shining. Every day is the magic place, and so we settle with the dust, pulling in sighs that last a whole night and exhale by morning.